THE GLORIES OF NATURE

FLOWERS

EDITED BY

RALPH L. WOODS

The Glories of Nature

FLOWERS

The World Publishing Company

NEW YORK AND

CLEVELAND

Published by World Publishing Company.
All rights reserved.

Published simultaneously in Canada
by Nelson, Foster & Scott, Ltd.

First printing—1971

Arranged and produced by Frank Fehmers Productions,
Amsterdam. An edition of the series "Buchers Miniaturen"
created by C.J. Bucher Publishers Ltd., Lucerne,
Switzerland, and first published in Switzerland.

Library of Congress Catalog Card Number: 78–152454

Printed in Switzerland.

WORLD PUBLISHING
TIMES MIRROR

Consider the lilies of the field,
    how they grow; they toil not,
        neither do they spin:
And yet I say unto you,
    That even Solomon in all his glory
        was not arrayed like one of these.

ST. MATTHEW 6:28-9

Flowers

How the universal heart of man blesses flowers!
They are wreathed round the cradle, the marriage-
altar, and the tomb. The Persian in the Far East
delights in their perfume, and writes his love in
nosegays; while the Indian child of the Far West
claps his hands with glee as he gathers the abundant
blossoms—the illuminated scriptures of the prairies.
The Cupid of the ancient Hindoo tipped his arrows
with flowers, and orange-flowers are a bridal crown
with us, a nation of yesterday.

Flowers garlanded the Grecian altar, and hung
in votive wreaths before the Christian shrine. All these
are appropriate uses. Flowers should deck the brow of
the youthful bride, for they are in themselves a lovely
type of marriage. The should twine round the tomb,
for their perpetually renewed beauty is a symbol of
the resurrection. They should festoon the altar, for
their fragrance and their beauty ascend in perpetual
worship before the Most High.

LYDIA MARIA CHILD

A Rain of Flowers

It is not raining rain for me,
    It's raining daffodils;
In every dimpled drop I see
    Wild flowers on the hills.

The clouds of gray engulf the day
    And overwhelm the town;
It is not raining rain to me,
    It's raining roses down.

It is not raining rain to me,
    But fields of clover bloom,
Where any buccaneering bee
    Can find a bed and room.

A health unto the happy,
    A fig for him who frets!
It is not raining rain to me,
    It's raining violets.

ROBERT LOVEMAN

Crocus Fire

It was the deep midnoon: one silvery cloud
Had lost his way between the piney sides
Of this long glen. Then to the bower they came . . .
And at their feet the crocus brake like fire . . .

ALFRED, LORD TENNYSON

Lowly, with a broken neck,
The crocus lays her cheek to mire.

GEORGE MEREDITH

Look how the blue-eyed violets glance love to one
   another!

T. B. READ

"A Blow of Tulips"

The gentleman of the house told me if I delighted in
flowers, it would be worth my while; for he believed
he could show me "such a blow of tulips as was not
to be matched in the whole country." I accepted
the offer. . . .

   I was very much pleased and astonished at the
glorious show of these gay vegetables, that arose in
great profusion on all the banks about us. Sometimes
I considered every leaf as an elaborate piece of tissue,
in which the threads and fibres were woven together
into different configurations, which gave a different
coloring to the light as it glanced on the several parts
of the surface. Sometimes I considered the whole bed
of tulips, according to the notion of the greatest
mathematician and philosopher that ever lived, as a
multitude of optic instruments, designed for
separating light into all those various colors of which
it is composed.

JOSEPH ADDISON

13

To Violets

Welcome maids of honor:
You do bring
In the Spring,
And wait upon her.

She has virgins many
Fresh and fair;
Yet you are
More sweet than any.

Y' are the maiden posies,
And so graced
To be placed
'Fore damask roses.

Yet though thus respected,
By-and-by
Ye do lie,
Poor girls, neglected.

ROBERT HERRICK

A violet by a mossy stone
Half hidden from the eye,
Fair as a star, when only one
Is shining in the sky.

WILLIAM WORDSWORTH

The Yellow Violet

Oft, in the sunless April day,
    Thy early smile has stayed my walk;
But midst the gorgeous blooms of May,
    I passed thee on thy humble stalk.

So they, who climb to wealth, forget
    The friends in darker fortunes tried.
I copied them—but I regret
    That I should ape the ways of pride.

And when again the genial hour
    Awakes the painted tribes of light,
I'll not o'er look the modest flower
    That made the woods of April bright.

WILLIAM CULLEN BRYANT

✦   ✦   ✦

Ye pretty daughters of the earth and sun.

WALTER RALEIGH

✦   ✦   ✦

Full-blown poppies, overcharged with rain
Decline the head, and drooping kiss the plain.

HOMER

15

Midsummer Pomp

Soon will the high Midsummer pomps come on,
    Soon will the musk carnations break the swell,
Soon shall we have gold-dusted snapdragon,
    Sweet William with his homely cottage-smell
And stocks in fragrant blow.

MATTHEW ARNOLD

And far and wide, in a scarlet tide,
The poppy's bonfire spread.

BAYARD TAYLOR

The Golden Poppy

The golden poppy is God's gold,
    The gold that lifts, nor weighs us down,
The gold that knows no miser's hold
    The gold that banks not in the town,
But singing, laughing, freely spills
Its hoard far up the happy hills;
Far up, far down, at every turn—
What beggar has not gold to burn!

JOAQUIN MILLER

Daisies, smell-less, yet most quaint,
  And sweet thyme true,
Primrose, first-born child of Ver,
Merry Spring-time's Harbinger.

JOHN FLETCHER

✓ ✓ ✓

Buttercups and daisies,
Oh, the pretty flowers;
Coming ere the Springtime
To tell of sunny hours.

MARY HOWITT

✓ ✓ ✓

Daisies, those pearled Arcturi of the earth,
The constellated flower that never sets.

PERCY BYSSHE SHELLEY

A Humble Friend

Small service is true service while it lasts,
Of humblest friends, bright creature! scorn not one;
The daisy, by the shadow that it casts,
Protects the lingering dewdrop from the sun.

WILLIAM WORDSWORTH

When daisies pied, and violets blue,
  And lady-smocks all silver-white,
And cuckoo-buds of yellow hue
  Do paint the meadows with delight.

WILLIAM SHAKESPEARE

✓　✓　✓

Full many a flower is born to blush unseen, and
waste its sweetness on the desert air.

THOMAS GRAY

Daisy's Song

The sun, with his great eye,
Sees not so much as I;
And the moon, all silver-proud,
Might as well be in a cloud.

And O the spring—the spring!
I lead the life of a king!
Couch'd in the teeming grass,
I spy each pretty lass.

I look where no one dares,
And I stare where no one stares,
And when the night is nigh,
Lambs bleat my lullaby.

JOHN KEATS

Shed no tear! O shed no tear!
The flower will bloom another year.
Weep no more! O weep no more!
Young buds sleep in the root's white core.

JOHN KEATS

Go, Lovely Rose

Go, lovely rose!
Tell her that wastes her time and me,
    That now she knows,
When I resemble her to thee,
How sweet and fair she seems to be.

Tell her, that's young,
And shuns to have her graces spied,
    That, hadst thou sprung
In deserts, where no men abide,
Thou must have uncommended died.

Small is the worth
Of beauty from the light retired;
    Bid her come forth,
Suffer herself to be desired,
And not blush so to be admired.

Then die! that she
The common fate of all things rare
    May read in thee,
How small a part of time they share
That are so wondrous sweet and fair!

EDMUND WALLER

And all the meadows, wide unrolled,
Were green and silver, green and gold,
Where buttercups and daisies spun
Their shining tissues in the sun.

JULIA C. R. DORR

Japanese Flower-Arranging

I have come to understand the unspeakable loveliness of a solitary spray of blossoms arranged as only a Japanese expert knows how to arrange it—not by simply poking the spray into a vase, but by perhaps one whole hour's labor of trimming and posing and daintiest manipulation—and therefore I cannot think now of what we Occidentals call a "bouquet" as anything but a vulgar murdering of flowers, an outrage upon the color-sense, a brutality, an abomination.

LAFCADIO HEARN

❧   ❧   ❧

Rose, thou art the sweetest flower
That ever drank the amber shower;
Rose, thou art the fondest child
Of dimpled Spring, the wood-nymph wild.

THOMAS MOORE

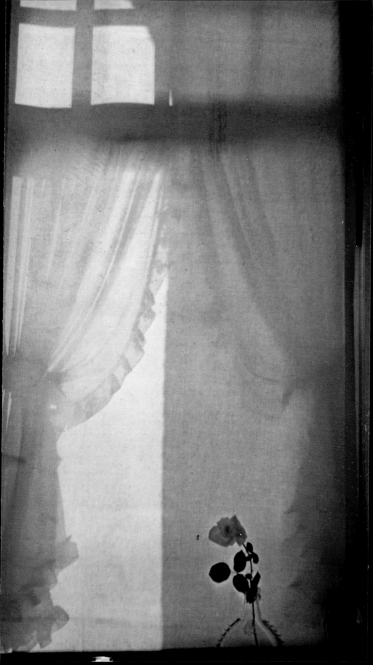

Gather ye rosebuds, while ye may,
Old Time is still a-flying:
And this same flower that smiles today,
Tomorrow will be dying.

ROBERT HERRICK

✦ ✦ ✦

Floral apostles! that in dewy splendor weep without
woe, and blush without a crime.

HORACE SMITH

✦ ✦ ✦

Loveliest of lovely things are they
On earth that soonest pass away.
The rose that lives its little hour
Is prized beyond the sculptured flower.

WILLIAM CULLEN BRYANT

✦ ✦ ✦

Two roses on one slender spray
In sweet communion grew,
Together hailed the morning ray
And drank the evening dew.

JAMES MONTGOMERY

The Personality of Flowers

Let long-lived pansies here their scents bestow,
The violet languish, and the roses glow;
In yellow glory let the crocus shine,
Narcissus here his love-sick head recline:
Here hyacinths in purple sweetness rise,
And tulips tinged with beauty's fairest dyes.

THOMAS BLACKLOCK

⚜   ⚜   ⚜

Lovely flowers are smiles of God's goodness.

SAMUEL WILBERFORCE

⚜   ⚜   ⚜

Flowers are the beautiful hieroglyphics of
nature, with which she indicates how much she
loves us.

J . W . VON GOETHE

⚜   ⚜   ⚜

Earth laughs in flowers.

RALPH WALDO EMERSON

The Columbine

One sometimes seems to discover a familiar wild
flower anew by coming upon it in some peculiar and
striking situation. Our columbine is at all times
and in all places one of the most exquisitely beautiful
of flowers; yet one spring day, when I saw it
growing out of a small seam on the face of a great
lichen-covered wall of rock, where no soil or mold
was visible—a jet of foliage and color shooting out
of a black line on the face of a perpendicular
mountain wall and rising up like a tiny fountain,
its drops turning to flame-colored jewels that hung
and danced in the air against the gray rocky surface
—its beauty became something magical and audacious.

JOHN BURROUGHS

Old-Fashioned Flowers

As for marigolds, poppies, hollyhocks, and
valorous sunflowers, we shall never have a garden
without them, both for their own sake, and for the
sake of old-fashioned folks, who used to love them.

HENRY WARD BEECHER

Multiple-Choice

I know not which I love the most,
    Nor which the comeliest shows,
The timid, bashful violet
    Or the royal-hearted rose:

The pansy in her purple dress,
    The pink with cheek of red,
Or the faint, fair heliotrope, who hangs,
    Like a bashful maid her head.

PHOEBE CARY

Flowers at Parade

See how the flowers, as at parade,
Under their colors stand displayed:
Each regiment in order grows,
That of the tulip, pink, and rose.

ANDREW MARVELL

What a desolate place would be a world without a flower! It would be a face without a smile, a feast without a welcome. Are not flowers the stars of the earth, and are not our stars the flowers of the heaven?

A. J. BALFOUR

The Flower

Once in a golden hour
 I cast to earth a seed.
Up there came a flower,
 The people said, a weed. . . .

Then it grew so tall
 It wore a crown of light,
But thieves from o'er the wall
 Stole the seed by night;

Sowed it far and wide
 By every town and tower,
Till all the people cried,
 "Splendid is the flower."

ALFRED, LORD TENNYSON

A Water-Lily at Evening

Sleep, lily, on the lake,
    Without one troubled dream
Thy hushed repose to break,
    Until the morning beam
Shall open thy glad heart again
To live its life apart from pain.

So still in thy repose,
    So pure thy petals seem,
As heaven would here disclose
    Its peace, and we might deem
A soul in each white lily lay
Passionless, from the lands of day.

F. W. BOURDILLON

The Fair Narcissus

The snowdrop, and then the violet,
Arose from the ground with warm rain wet,
And their breath was mixed with fresh odour, sent
From the turf, like the voice and the instrument.

Then the pied wind-flowers and the tulip tall,
And narcissi, the fairest among them all,
Who gaze on their eyes in the stream's recess,
Till they die of their own dear loveliness.

PERCY BYSSHE SHELLEY

A Radiant Vision

If we had never before looked upon the earth,
but suddenly came to it man or woman grown, set
down in the midst of a summer mead, would it
not seem to us a radiant vision? . . . So it seemed
to me as a boy, sweet and new like this each
morning.

RICHARD JEFFRIES

Here are sweet peas, on tip-toe for a flight:
With wings of gentle flush o'er delicate white,
And taper fingers catching at all things,
To bind them all about with tiny rings.

JOHN KEATS

To the Fringed Gentian

Thou blossom, bright with autumn dew,
    And colored with the heaven's own blue,
That openest when the quiet light
Succeeds the keen and frosty night;

Thou comest not when the violets lean
O'er wandering brooks and springs unseen,
Or columbines, in purple dressed,
Nor o'er the ground-bird's hidden nest.

Thou waitest late, and com'st alone,
When woods are bare and birds are flown,
And frost and shortening days portend
The aged Year is near his end.

Then doth thy sweet and quiet eye
Look through its fringes to the sky,
Blue—blue—as if that sky let fall
A flower from its cerulean wall.

WILLIAM CULLEN BRYANT

May-Flower

Pink, small, and punctual,
Aromatic, low,
Covert in April,
Candid in May.

Dear to the moss,
Known by the knoll,
Next to the robin
In every human soul.

Bold little beauty,
Bedecked with thee,
Nature foreswears
Antiquity.

EMILY DICKINSON

＊　＊　＊

O rose! the sweetest blossom,
Of spring the fairest flower,
O rose! the joy of heaven.
The god of love, with roses
His yellow locks adorning,
Dances with the hours and graces.

J. G. PERCIVAL

"The Garden's Pride"

If on creation's morn the king of heaven
To shrubs and flowers a sovereign lord had given,
O beauteous rose, he had anointed thee
Of shrubs and flowers the sovereign lord to be;
The spotless emblem of unsullied truth,
The smile of beauty and the flow of youth,
The garden's pride, the grace of vernal bowers,
The blush of meadows, and the eye of flowers.

H. G. BOHN

✐   ✐   ✐

You love the roses—so do I. I wish
The sky would rain down roses, as they rain
From off the shaken bush. Why will it not?
Then all the valleys would be pink and white,
And soft to tread on. They would fall as light
As feathers, smelling sweet; and it would be
Like sleeping and yet be, waking all at once,
Over the sea, Queen, where we soon shall go,
Will it rain roses?

GEORGE ELIOT

Central depth of purple,
    Leaves more bright than rose,
Who shall tell her what brightest thought
    Out of darkness grows?

LEIGH HUNT

✔   ✔   ✔

Yet mark'd I where the bolt of Cupid fell:
It fell upon a little western flower,
Before milk-white, now purple with love's wound
And maidens call it Love-in-idleness.

WILLIAM SHAKESPEARE

Marigolds

Open afresh your round of starry folds,
Ye ardent marigolds!
Dry up the moisture from your golden lids,
For great Apollo bids
That in these days your praises should be sung
On many harps, which he has lately strung;
And when again your dewiness he kisses,
Tell him, I have you in my world of blisses:
So haply when I rove in some far vale,
His mighty voice may come upon the gale.

JOHN KEATS

Thoughts in a Garden

How snowdrops cold, and blue-eyed harebells, blend
Their tender tears, as o'er the streams they bend;
The love-sick violet, and the primrose pale,
Bow their sweet heads, and whisper to the gale;
With secret sighs the virgin lily droops,
And jealous cowslips hang their tawny cups.
How the young rose, in beauty's damask pride,
Drinks the warm blushes of his bashful bride;
With honey lips enamoured woodbines meet,
Clasp with fond arms, and mix their kisses sweet.

ERASMUS DARWIN

Gathering a Nosegay

During the months of September and October
I never collected a nosegay which took me less than
three hours of seeking, I was so lost in admiration—
with the mild indolence of a poet—of these transient
allegories which represented to me the strongest
contrasts of human life, majestic scenes in which
my memory now digs for treasure. To this day I often
wed to such grand spectacles my remembrance of the
soul that then pervaded nature. I still see in them
my Queen, whose white dress floated through the
copse and danced over the lawns, and whose spirit
came up to me like a promise of fruition from every
flower cup of amorous stamens.

No declaration, no proof of unbounded passion
was ever more contagious than were these symphonies
of flowers, wherein my cheated desires gave me such
inspiration as Beethoven could express in notes.

HONORÉ DE BALZAC

✼   ✼   ✼

Here's flowers for you:
Hot lavender, mints, savory, marjoram,
The marigold that goes to bed with the sun
And with him rises weeping.

WILLIAM SHAKESPEARE

53

Autumn Flowers

Those few pale autumn flowers,
How beautiful they are!
Than all that went before,
Than all the summer's store,
How lovelier far!

And why? They are the last—
The last!—the last!—the last!—
Oh, by that little word,
How many thoughts are stirred!
That whisper of the past!

Pale flowers!—pale, perishing flowers!
Ye're types of precious things,—
Types of those bitter moments
That flit, like life's enjoyments,
On rapid, rapid wings.

CAROLINE ANNE SOUTHEY

A Bouquet

Flowers to the fair: to you these flowers I bring,
And strive to greet you with an earlier spring.
Flowers sweet, and gay, and delicate like you;
Emblems of innocence, and beauty too.
With flowers the Graces bind their yellow hair,
And flowery wreaths consenting lovers wear.
Flowers, the sole luxury which nature knew,
In Eden's pure and guiltless garden grew. . . .
Gay without toil, and lovely without art,
They spring to cheer the sense and glad the heart.
Nor blush, my fair, to own you copy these;
Your best, your sweetest empire is—to please.

ANNA LETITIA BARBAULD